As one of the world's longest established and best-known travel brands, Thomas Cook are the experts in travel.

For more than 135 years our guidebooks have unlocked the secrets of destinations around the world, sharing with travellers a wealth of experience and a passion for travel.

Rely on Thomas Cook as your travelling companion on your next trip and benefit from our unique heritage.

Thomas Cook **pocket** guides

NORWICH

Your travelling companion since 1873

Written by Lucy Armstrong

Published by Thomas Cook Publishing
A division of Thomas Cook Tour Operations Limited
Company registration no. 3772199 England
The Thomas Cook Business Park, Unit 9, Coningsby Road,
Peterborough PE3 8SB, United Kingdom
Email: books@thomascook.com, Tel: +44 (0) 1733 416477
www.thomascookpublishing.com

Produced by Cambridge Publishing Management Limited
Burr Elm Court, Main Street, Caldecote CB23 7NU
www.cambridgepm.co.uk

ISBN: 978-1-84848-491-7

This first edition © 2011 Thomas Cook Publishing
Text © Thomas Cook Publishing
Cartography supplied by Redmoor Design, Tavistock, Devon
Map data © OpenStreetMap contributors CC-BY-SA, www.openstreetmap.org,
www.creativecommons.org

Series Editor: Karen Beaulah
Production/DTP: Steven Collins

Printed and bound in Spain by GraphyCems

Cover photography © travelbild.com/Alamy

CONTENTS

SYMBOLS KEY

The following symbols are used throughout this book:

ⓐ address **ⓣ** telephone **ⓦ** website address **ⓔ** email
ⓛ opening times **ⓝ** public transport connections **ⓘ** important

The following symbols are used on the maps:

ⓘ information office		▪ point of interest	
✈ airport		O city	
➕ hospital		O large town	
🛡 police station		○ small town	
🚌 bus station		= motorway	
🚆 railway station		— main road	
🛍 shopping		— minor road	
✝ cathedral		— railway	
✉ post office		P+🚍 park & ride	
❶ numbers denote featured cafés, restaurants & venues			

PRICE CATEGORIES

The ratings below indicate average price rates for a double
room per night, including breakfast:

£ up to £60   **££** £60–120   **£££** over £120

The typical cost for a three-course meal without drinks,
is as follows:

£ up to £15   **££** £15–25   **£££** over £25

ⓞ *Norwich Cathedral in late summer*

4

INTRODUCING
Norwich

Introduction

Norwich may have a long history, but it's certainly not stuck in the past. Medieval in parts but modern in outlook, it's home to a growing student-turned-young-professional population who, once their studies are over, never quite get around to leaving. And it's easy to see why. With one foot in the past and another firmly rooted in the present, Norwich is everything a city should be – energetic yet chilled, compact but never claustrophobic, dressed in historical detail but with a fresh, modern vibe.

This marriage of old and new is thanks to, in part, Norwich's emerging status as a destination for culture. Visitors have always been attracted by its history – architecturally evident all around – but, today, culture vultures are flocking to Norfolk too. With an impressive calendar of annual events, which includes the Norfolk and Norwich Festival, the city isn't shy about attracting newcomers; and yet the cultural calendar never feels staged – the residents of Norfolk and Norwich enjoy the city just as much as those who visit.

There's a strong religious presence (Norwich is one of only a few cities that can boast two cathedrals), but there's also plenty of fun to be had. The people of Norwich are a lively lot and a long pattern of resistance may account for the indomitable spirit that you'll recognise today. But, although rebellion runs deep, the residents are also friendly and you'll no doubt experience some of their warmth during your stay – whether asking for directions or settling down for an ale or two (brewed locally, of course) in a city pub.

And, if that wasn't enough, the countryside is never far away either. Upon leaving the city, the county quickly becomes rural and, if you're yearning for the great outdoors, you don't have far to go. Boasting a spectacular coastline and Britain's largest wetland, there's no compromise when you visit Norwich – you really can have it all. Today, Norwich is an evolving modern city with a perfect blend of history, culture, shopping and entertainment. It's fresh and it's exciting – and you might just be surprised by what you find.

🔺 *The Forum: Norwich's landmark millennium building*

When to go

SEASONS & CLIMATE

There's never a bad time to visit Norwich. During the winter you can cosy up in one of the many cafés, warm yourself with a pint and a pie and enjoy the city in all its festive glory. As the weather warms up, Norwich becomes the perfect base for exploring all the region has to offer. Culturally, the highlight of the year is the Norfolk and Norwich Festival and it's a great excuse to visit.

ANNUAL EVENTS

The turning on of the Christmas lights (usually a Thursday night in November) marks the beginning of the **festive season** in Norwich. Your Christmas shopping needs will be answered by the markets that spring up over the main **Haymarket/Gentleman's Walk** thoroughfare and, in December, tonnes of magnificently carved blocks of ice arrive in the city centre for the **ice sculpture trail**.

The University of East Anglia (UEA) hosts two annual bookish events: the **Spring Literary Festival** and the **Autumn Literary Festival**. The UEA is renowned for its famous Creative Writing Course (past students include Ian McEwan, Kazuo Ishiguro, Tracy Chevalier and John Boyne), so it's little wonder that their festivals attract some big-name authors. For the latest news, authors and dates visit ⓦ www.uea.ac.uk/litfest; to book tickets go to ⓦ www.ueaticketbookings.co.uk or telephone ① 01603 508050.

Also in the spring, the **Norfolk & Norwich Festival** is a celebration of music, dance, theatre and art and one of the UK's biggest city festivals. The streets become a stage for outdoor performances and temporary installations, and even if you haven't booked anything it's impossible not to get caught up in the excitement. ⓦ www.nnfestival.org.uk

The highlight of the **Lord Mayor's Celebration** in July is the Lord Mayor's Procession, followed by fireworks and further entertainment at **Chapelfield Gardens**, while the **Norfolk Food Festival** turns the city, and the county, into a gastronome's delight during September. ⓦ www.norfolkfoodfestival.co.uk

The annual **Norwich Beer Festival**, in October, is a great chance to visit the magnificent 15th-century St Andrew's Hall. The people of Norwich are a thirsty lot, so be prepared for queues if you choose to visit in the evening. ⓦ www.norwichcamra.org.uk

⬤ *Norwich Castle is popular all year round*

History

Over the centuries, Norwich has been marked by numerous settlements. What is known today as Norfolk used to be an area inhabited by the Iceni people, whose famous leader, Boudica, led an unsuccessful revolt against the Romans. The Romans settled the territory next and stayed for more than 300 years. They were followed by the Vikings, the Danes and the Saxons, none of whom left significant marks on the city.

The Normans were the first to do so. When they arrived in Norwich around the 11th century, they inherited a significant

⬥ *Dragon Hall*

and populous city, architectural memories of which are still evident today. Begun in 1067, the Norman castle continues to stand proudly over the city, and just a few minutes' walk away you'll find Norwich Cathedral, another Norman landmark dating from the same time.

Work on the city walls began during the Middle Ages and their remains can still be found at several points on the city outskirts today. It was a prosperous time for the city thanks, in part, to a flourishing wool trade. Unfortunately, however, it was also a time of death – due to the arrival of the Plague in Norwich.

Under the Tudors, land traditionally available for farming and grazing was being 'enclosed' by landowners. In 1549 some townsfolk from Wymondham began tearing down enclosure fences; rebels and Robert Kett, a landowner himself, joined the men before they could turn on him. Kett led the 16,000-strong group towards the city where they were eventually defeated by foreign troops. Thousands of Kett's men were killed in battle and Kett himself suffered a rather gruesome death at the top of Norwich Castle. His hanged body was left there as a decaying warning to any would-be rebels.

During the Georgian and Victorian periods, some of the city's key industries set up shop. The first incarnation of Norwich Union was founded in 1797 and in 1814 Colman's Mustard came on to the scene.

The city's characteristic independent streak is still evident today. Along with Exeter, Norwich Council had been hoping to secure unitary rule. However, its dreams of 'home rule' seem likely to be blocked by the coalition government.

Culture

Norwich's cultural scene is modern, vibrant and constantly evolving. A poignant focal point for this cultural activity is the **Sainsbury Centre for Visual Arts**, located in the grounds of the university (ⓐ UEA ❶ 01603 593199 ⓦ www.scva.org.uk ⓔ scva@uea.ac.uk ⓛ 10.00–17.00 Tues–Sun, closed Mon ⓝ Bus: 23, 35). Housed in a magnificent glass-fronted hangar-style building designed in the mid-1970s by a then relatively unknown Norman Foster, this is the perfect setting for some fascinating temporary exhibitions.

The recently refurbished **Theatre Royal** (see page 51) is often a stop on national touring circuits, and it welcomes a diverse range of performances. For something a bit cosier, head to **The Maddermarket** (ⓐ St John's Alley ❶ 01603 620917 ⓦ www. maddermarket.co.uk). **Norwich Playhouse** (ⓐ 42–58 St George's Street ❶ 01603 612580 ⓦ www.norwichplayhouse.org.uk) also stages a number of plays, as well as comedy. DJ Adam Buxton's BUG nights are a local favourite (see page 67).

CITY OF CULTURE
Norwich may have lost out to Derry for the City of Culture 2013 title but, with characteristic defiance, it has vowed to celebrate anyway. To find out more about what's planned for 2013 visit ⓦ www.norwichcityofculture.co.uk

▶ *Elm Hill at dusk*

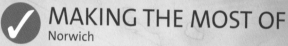

MAKING THE MOST OF
Norwich

Shopping

From an Art Nouveau arcade to England's largest six-day market, there's a diverse range of shopping experiences to be had in Norwich, along with all the usual high-street offerings.

With almost 200 stalls, the colourful rooftops of **Norwich Market** have become an iconic city image (ⓐ Haymarket ⓦ www.norwich-market.co.uk). Even if you're not interested in its wares, which range from food to clothes, from hardware to jewellery, it's worth finding a route in and getting among the action – although it may be more difficult finding your way out of the hustle and bustle!

As well as enjoying the permanent delights of Norwich Market, you may be lucky enough to be in town for one of a range of temporary shopping experiences. **St Andrew's Hall** regularly hosts arts and crafts and antiques and collectors' fairs. The cloister provides a beautiful backdrop to the wares on display. Indeed, if your tastes are for the old rather than the new, head down to **Tombland Antiques Centre**, which calls the beautiful Augustine Steward House home (ⓐ 14 Tombland).

If you prefer your shopping a bit more mainstream, then you'll find all the high-street favourites along the main **Gentleman's Walk/Haymarket** thoroughfare, **St Stephen's Street** and at **Chapelfield Mall**. Chapelfield is a fairly recent addition to the shopping scene. Built where the Nestlé factory once stood, the mall opened in 2005.

If you want to find something that you couldn't find in any other UK city, then bypass the high street and head for the **Norwich Lanes**. Nestled in the twists and turns of the cobbled streets beyond the Guildhall are funky fashion outlets, cool jewellery shops and inviting cafés. Geographically, the Norwich Lanes area doesn't discriminate – it encompasses the cobbled, mostly pedestrianised, streets around **Pottergate** and **Lower Goat Lane**, but seems to be ever-expanding into the areas beyond.

🔺 *Victorian grandeur in the Royal Arcade*

Eating & drinking

Once you've had your fill of history, culture and shopping, there are plenty of places to satisfy your hunger and thirst, whatever your tastes.

When the cafés begin to shut up for the day, the pubs start to fill – and if you're a fan of real ale this is where the fun really starts. The beer hasn't come from too far away – local favourites include Adnams (brewed at Southwold in Suffolk) and Woodfordes (at Woodbastwick, just a few miles out of the city). Several pubs brew their own – the **Coach and Horses** on Thorpe Road is home to the Chalk Hill Brewery and local brewers Grain Brewery recently opened their first pub, **The Plough**, on St Benedict's.

But, for a real experience you'll need to walk out of the city centre and head towards the **Fat Cat** (ⓐ Nelson Street, off Dereham Road ⓦ www.fatcatpub.co.uk ⓛ 12.00–23.00 Mon–Fri & Sun, 11.00–23.00 Sat). Sample the real-ale menu and you'll see why it was awarded *The Good Pub Guide*'s Beer Pub of the Year 2010.

Norwich also has some fantastic restaurants dotted around the city centre and beyond. All cuisines are catered for, whether you fancy Italian, Thai, French or Indian-inspired food. Specialities of the region include Norfolk poultry, Cromer crabs, Colman's mustard, mussels from Stiffkey and Sheringham shrimp and lobster. There are a number of excellent farm shops and delicatessens both in Norwich itself and on the coast, at Holkham and Cley, among other places.

🔺 *Relaxing with a drink at Take 5*

Entertainment

Whatever your idea of a good night out is, you'll be able to have one in Norwich. The city's culture doesn't disappear when the sun goes down and there are plenty of places to visit to get your fill of good music, art, cinema or theatre.

If you prefer your music live rather than through a sound system or delivered by a DJ, then check out what's on at the **Norwich Arts Centre** during your stay. It's an incredible venue and bands seem to enjoy playing there as much as the audiences enjoy hearing them – apparently the novelty of making noise in a church has never really worn off for anyone!

If you're dying to unpack your glad rags, then you'll find music, dancing and general mayhem from **Prince of Wales Road** down to **Riverside**. Prince of Wales Road is lined with bars and clubs and the Riverside development (off Koblenz Avenue) is home to restaurants, a cinema, a bowling alley and some more

EVENTS LISTINGS

Keep up to date with what's happening during your stay with the **Eastern Daily Press** (ⓦ www.edp24.co.uk), its sister paper the **Evening News** (ⓦ www.eveningnews24.co.uk) or, for a more entertaining and discursive take on things, **Outline** (ⓦ www.outlineonline.co.uk). The UEA website has information and a booking facility for its own events as well as those taking place at various venues throughout the city, including the Waterfront and Norwich Arts Centre.

bars. It's loud and it's brash and if that's what you want, that's where you'll find it.

If you've packed your indie dancing shoes, then hotfoot it across the footbridge from Riverside and dance the night away at **The Waterfront** (ⓐ King Street ❶ 01603 508050 ⓦ www.waterfrontnorwich.com). Check their website to see what club nights are on and who's playing while you're here.

△ *Cinema City (see page 65)*

Sport & relaxation

SPECTATOR SPORTS

Carrow Road is not only home to **Norwich City Football Club**
(ⓦ www.canaries.co.uk), but also to celebrity chef Delia Smith's
city restaurant (ⓦ www.deliascanarycatering.com).

⬥ *Carrow Road: home of Norwich City Football Club, known as the Canaries*

PARTICIPATION SPORTS

The **Sportspark** at the UEA (Ⓦ www.sportspark.co.uk ⓣ 01603 592398) has a gym, swimming pool, badminton and squash courts, aerobics classes and Norfolk's tallest climbing wall.

For golfers, there are plenty of courses where you can practise your swing. **Dunston Hall** is situated just outside the city centre and also has a spa and restaurant within the hotel (ⓐ Ipswich Road ⓣ 01508 470444 Ⓦ www.devere.co.uk/our-locations/dunston-hall). **Sprowston Manor**, north of the city, has a similar offering. ⓐ Wroxham Road ⓣ 01603 410871 Ⓦ www.marriott.co.uk

RELAXATION

Even if you're looking for a slightly less active break in Norwich, there is plenty on offer. Grab a picnic lunch and spend a lazy afternoon in **Earlham Park**, close to the UEA, or Eaton Park, where you can burn off your picnic with a game of pitch and putt.

If your idea of relaxation is a bit more indulgent, then head to a city spa. **The Lemon Tree** (ⓐ Woburn Court ⓣ 01603 219264) is conveniently located in the city centre, tucked away behind Guildhall Hill; at **Ritual Day Spa** (ⓐ Exchange Street ⓣ 01603 623366 Ⓦ www.ritualdayspa.co.uk) you can indulge for as little or as long as you want (they even offer 12-month packages) and, if all this relaxation leaves you feeling peckish, at **Thai Wellbeing** (ⓐ 19/25 Red Lion Street ⓣ 01603 666050 Ⓦ www.thaiwellbeing.co.uk) you can follow your treatment with a **Thai meal** in the restaurant next door.

And don't forget the therapeutic qualities of a dose of sea air – the Norfolk coast is only a short journey away.

Accommodation

Accommodation options in Norwich cater for all tastes and budgets. If you'd prefer to spend your money on enjoying the sights, culture, restaurants and pubs in Norwich, then there are several options. **Travelodge** (ⓦ www.travelodge.co.uk) often works out the cheapest and there's one in the city centre on St Stephen's Street and another on Vedast Street, just behind Prince of Wales Road. **Premier Inn** (ⓦ www.premierinn.com) has a hotel located at the bottom of Prince of Wales Road or, for a quieter location, there's also one on Duke Street.

As well as the usual chain offerings, there are some lovely boutique-style hotels and modern, comfortable B&Bs, where you can stay in the city centre but feel as if you're a million miles away from the hustle and bustle of a modern city.

HOTELS & GUESTHOUSES

The Langtry Rooms £ The Langtry Rooms are just outside the city centre, in the heart of the 'golden triangle' – making them perfectly situated if you want to sample some of the pubs around this area. In fact, you won't have to go too far because the rooms are run by, and just across the road from, The Langtry pub – which serves reasonably priced food and drink. ⓐ 82 Unthank Road ⓣ 01603 469347 ⓦ www.thelangtry.co.uk ⓔ bookings@thelangtryrooms.co.uk

Beeches Hotel £–££ The Beeches is actually made up of three separate buildings – the Beeches, Governor's Lodge and Plantation House. All stand in the shadow of the

Roman Catholic cathedral, next to the Plantation Garden. Depending on your budget, there is a variety of rooms available across the three different locations. The Governor's Lodge is the cheapest option and for the best prices check their website first. If you find yourself staying in this area of town, then pop across the road to the Workshop for some tasty tapas and home-cooked pizza. ❸ 2–6 Earlham Road ❶ 01603 621167 Ⓦ www.beecheshotelnorwich.co.uk Ⓔ info@beecheshotelnorwich.co.uk

3 Princes Street ££ Carol has opened up her beautiful family home to visitors, a stone's throw from the city centre and just around the corner from Elm Hill. You'll find three nicely decorated bedrooms and a relaxed, laid-back atmosphere. Your hostess will bring breakfast upstairs for you and you can enjoy it in your room while planning the day ahead. ❸ 3 Princes Street ❶ 01603 662693 Ⓦ www.3princes-norwich.co.uk Ⓔ hardman@3princes-norwich.co.uk

Number 17 ££ In a peaceful location, yet only a short walk from the city centre, Number 17 boasts modern, comfortable rooms. The family rooms – on two levels – are a treat if you're bringing the kids along. There's a nice communal space, where breakfast is served, plus a hot tub and courtyard garden so you can really unwind. ❸ Colegate ❶ 01603 764486 Ⓦ www.number17norwich.co.uk Ⓔ enquiries@number17norwich.co.uk

By Appointment ££–£££ For something a bit different, the rooms at By Appointment offer a unique sleeping experience.

Bursting with character and charm, the regally named bedrooms in this 15th-century building come complete with antique details. It's a lovely part of town in which to base yourself. ⓐ 25–29 St George's Street ⓣ 01603 630730 ⓦ www.byappointmentnorwich.co.uk

Maids Head Hotel ££–£££ Just past Tombland, at the tip of Magdalen Street, the Maids Head is well located within the shadow of the cathedral. The large 13th-century building houses over 80 bedrooms and a restaurant, with conference and wedding facilities. Apparently, Elizabeth I also put her head down here, so you'd be in good company. ⓐ Tombland ⓣ 01603 209966 ⓦ www.maidsheadhotel.co.uk

Georgian House Hotel £££ Situated on the city-centre side of Unthank Road, the Georgian House Hotel is just a short walk from the centre, and also home to The Mirror Bar and Rare Grill and Steakhouse – so you don't need to go far for a drink or some food. Thanks to a recent refurbishment, the 30 en-suite rooms are nicely decorated and comfortable. ⓐ 30–34 Unthank Road ⓣ 01603 615655 ⓦ www.georgian-hotel.co.uk

St Giles House Hotel £££ The grandeur of the St Giles House's exterior hints at the luxury and attention to detail that you'll find inside. From double rooms to suites, there's something for everyone – at a price. If you really want to treat yourself, book one of the de-luxe suites and schedule some pampering time at the hotel spa. ⓐ 41–45 St Giles Street ⓣ 01603 275180 ⓦ www.stgileshousehotel.com

STAYING ON A BOAT

Barnes Brinkcraft £–£££ Whether you're after a boat for a day or longer, there's a range of craft available at Barnes Brinkcraft in Wroxham to suit your needs. ☎ 01603 782625 ⓦ www.barnesbrinkcraft.co.uk

Posh Boats £££ Holiday on the Broads in style in a posh boat – complete with LCD TV, Wi-Fi, Molton Brown toiletries, slippers and champagne. Leave your prejudices about boating holidays at the moorside and jump on board for an unforgettable experience. ☎ 01508 499167 ⓦ www.poshboats.co.uk ⓔ enquiries@poshboats.co.uk

▲ *Messing about in boats on Malthouse Broad*

THE BEST OF NORWICH

Whether you are in Norwich for a day or a week, and your taste is for history, culture, live music, good food or real ale, there's something here to suit everyone and every taste.

TOP 10 ATTRACTIONS

- **Norwich Cathedral** No trip to Norwich is complete without a visit to this magnificent landmark and the peaceful Cathedral Close which it calls home (see pages 60–63).

- **Riverside Walk** For a view of the city away from the centre, enjoy an amble down the Wensum – taking in Cow Tower and Pulls Ferry (see pages 63–4).

- **Norwich and Norfolk Festival** Time your visit to coincide with this popular festival and see the city transformed into a hub of cultural activity and entertainment (see pages 8–9).

- **Norfolk Broads** Use Norwich as the perfect base for discovering the rest of Norfolk's beautiful countryside and England's biggest wetland (see pages 84–8).

- **Shrine of St Julian** Take time to visit the resting place of this local saint and pick up your copy of the first English book written by a female (see page 50).

- **Norwich Castle** The beautiful Norman keep is a perfect setting for discovering the history of the city and admiring its artistic endeavours (see pages 47–8).

- **Ghost Walk** Take a walk on the wild side and uncover Norwich's spooky secrets with the Man in Black (see pages 66–7).

- **Elm Hill** Step back in time and walk the cobbles of Tudor England in one of the city's best preserved streets (see page 60).

- **South Asian Decorative Arts Collection** Enjoy a taste of the exotic in the heart of the city with a trip to this beautifully colourful space (see pages 51–2).

- **Retail therapy** Don your comfiest shoes and explore the retail heaven of Chapelfield Mall and the Royal Arcade (see page 14).

🔻 *Pulls Ferry*

Suggested itineraries

HALF DAY: NORWICH IN A HURRY

If you've only got a couple of hours in the city then don't worry about fitting everything in – once you've had a taster of Norwich you're bound to be back for a longer stay. But, in the meantime, to get the best of the city in just a few hours, pop into the **cathedral** and take a leisurely walk around the beautiful **Cathedral Close**. **Elm Hill** is just a couple of minutes away – stop at **Olive's** (see page 70) for a quick caffeine fix and walk up the medieval street back towards the city.

1 DAY: TIME TO SEE A LITTLE MORE

Once you've visited the cathedral and Elm Hill, complete your history of the city with a trip to **Norwich Castle**. Join a tour of the battlements for a spectacular view across Norwich and come back down again to get ready for a night out. Enjoy some evening drinks at the **Rumsey Wells** and **The Plough** (see pages 73–4) and then stroll up into the city for a delicious Thai dinner at **The Vine** (see page 58). If you want to make the most of your 24 hours in the city, then head to **Tombland** for some post-dinner cocktails.

2–3 DAYS: SHORT CITY BREAK

With a few days to enjoy the city you can intersperse the sightseeing with some shopping, café visits and pretty city walks. Take a break from the hustle and bustle and enjoy a walk along the **River Wensum**, taking in **Cow Tower** and **Pulls Ferry** (see pages 63–4). Pay a visit to **St John's Cathedral** (see page 44) on the other side of the city and, while you're there, spend an hour or two admiring the handiwork of Victorian philanthropist Henry Trevor at the **Plantation Garden** (see page 48). Try to take in a live performance at the **Norwich Arts Centre**, **Playhouse** (see pages 66 and 67) or **The Waterfront** (see page 59).

LONGER: ENJOYING NORWICH TO THE FULL

A longer stay means you have the opportunity not only to enjoy everything Norwich has to offer but also to make it out to the **Broads** and the **Norfolk coast** (see pages 76–88). Whether you fancy hiring a boat, chilling on the beach or taking a long walk, complement your city break with a good dose of fresh air and see what the rest of Norfolk has to offer.

● *Cathedral Close*

Something for nothing

Absorbing the history and culture of Norwich won't cost you a penny. From medieval **Elm Hill** to the modern **Forum**, Norwich is a city of diverse beauty – and it costs nothing to admire.

You can step back in time without visiting any museum with a trip to Elm Hill. The cobbled street is home to Tudor buildings and adorable little shops (well, it costs nothing to window shop). It's also a good place to see the **River Wensum** (see pages 63–4). You can continue to follow the river from here and join the **Riverside Walk**, which shows off some beautiful, quieter, parts of the city.

Both cathedrals are also free to visit and, at the **Anglican Cathedral** (see pages 60–63), it's easy to while away an afternoon with a good book in the peaceful **Cathedral Close** – although it will take some confidence to walk past the till and attendant and straight into the cathedral without 'donating'.

If a riverside walk and the peace and tranquillity of the cathedral leave you yearning for some city-centre action, then the **South Asian Decorative Arts and Crafts Collection** (see pages 51–2) is free to visit, and it's just around the corner from one of the city's landmark architectural details – **The Forum** (see pages 45–7). Swing buy and visit **Fusion** (see page 46), where you can admire Europe's largest digital screen gallery – for nothing.

If you can stretch your budget to £1, then it's possible to visit **Norwich Castle** (see pages 47–8) if you go an hour before closing (or between 12.00 and 13.00 on term-time weekdays). You won't be able to have the full experience, so just pick an area of interest and spend a leisurely hour there.

When it rains

It's always wise to bring a brolly on a city break in the UK and, weather-wise, to prepare for the worst. If you're stranded at the beach, then poor weather may hold you back but, in the city, there is plenty to keep you busy – and dry – while the rain clouds pass.

You can easily get the most out of your admission charge to **Norwich Castle** (see pages 47–8) – there's plenty to keep you busy for hours on end. The fee includes a visit to the **Royal Norfolk Regimental Museum** (see pages 48–9), which can be accessed from the castle, so there's no need to face the elements as you navigate between the two. But, if you've already done the sights, then splash your holiday cash at **Chapelfield** (see pages 53–4). There are two floors of shopping (plus a food and drinks floor) – so even the worst of storms will have passed by the time you're done.

For a few cosy hours away from the worst of the elements, grab a glass of wine, a hot chocolate or a real ale and catch a film at **Cinema City** (see page 65). You'll soon relax into the comfy seats and, with your beverage of choice in hand, you can spend a lovely afternoon warm and tucked away from the outside world.

If you needed one, then a spot of rain is a great excuse to indulge in the city's café culture. **Frank's Bar** (see pages 55–6) is a good stop any time of the day or, if you fancy something a bit stronger, then a pint (or two) of real ale at the **Fat Cat** (see page 16) will give you a warm glow and help you forget the miserable weather outside.

On arrival

ARRIVING

By air
Norwich International is a small airport situated about five miles from the city centre on the ring road, with all the usual facilities you'd expect (although perhaps slightly smaller than you're used to). It receives arrivals from cities throughout the UK as well as Europe and, thanks to the connection with Schiphol airport, many more destinations worldwide. **Norwich Airport Taxis** (☏ 01603 424044) are waiting outside the terminal to take you to your destination. A cheaper option is bus 27, which will drop you off in the city.

By rail
The rather grand-looking railway station is situated near the Riverside area of the city, about a 10- to 15-minute walk from the city centre. Taxis will be waiting outside the station, and there's a bus stop just past the taxi rank with bus 25 taking you into the city. If you're not weighed down with too much luggage, it's an easy walk into the centre – cross the bridge and continue up Prince of Wales Road. Turn right towards Tombland and then left on to Queen Street. Cross Redwell Street on to London Street and you'll be in the centre of Norwich.

By road
The A11 is the main road into the county and it can get clogged up around Elveden, particularly at the weekends. The A11 will take you down Newmarket Road and straight into the city centre. Or, if

◆ *Norwich Railway Station*

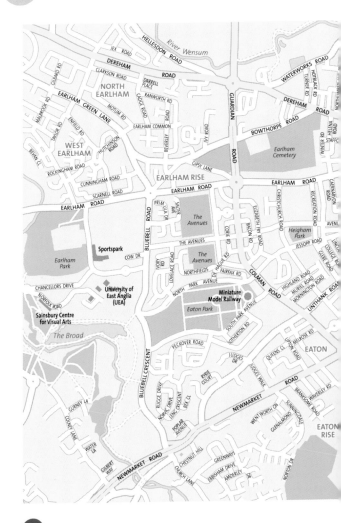

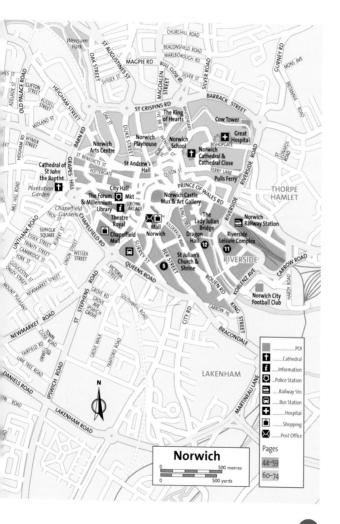

Norwich

| | 0 | 500 metres |
| 0 | 500 yards |

Legend:

- POI
- Cathedral
- Information
- Police Station
- Railway Stn
- Bus Station
- Hospital
- Shopping
- Post Office

Pages
44–59
60–74

35

you're coming from the east coast or from the Midlands, then you'll arrive along the A47. Follow the signs to Norwich, or leave the A47 at Thickthorn to connect with the A11.

If you want to avoid the city centre, then there are two ring roads that radiate around Norwich – the inner ring road (St Crispins, Barrack Street, Riverside Road, Queen's Road, Chapelfield Road and Grapes Hill) and the outer ring road (A140 and A1042).

Finding somewhere to park in any city can be stressful. In Norwich, it's probably easiest to head straight to a multi-storey. **Chapelfield Mall** has its own underground car park off Chapelfield Road, and the **Mall Norwich** has two – a small one off Farmers Avenue and the main one off Market Avenue. **St Andrew's**, on Duke Street, is another good option. The main car parks, with the number of spaces available, are signposted on your approach to the city centre so you should be able to find one with little trouble.

FINDING YOUR FEET

Norwich is a friendly and relatively safe city, but, as in any city, it's important to remain vigilant and aware of your surroundings. The **Tourist Information Centre** (see page 93) is located in the glass-fronted **Forum** building, just beyond Gentleman's Walk – you'll sneak a peek of it to your left, in between Next and Starbucks, as you're walking along the main thoroughfare.

Between April and October the open-top **city sightseeing bus** is a good way to become familiar with the city (☎ 01263 587005 🌐 www.awaydays.com/norwich-tours.htm). If you'd prefer to acquaint yourself with the city on the waterways, then **City Boats** (⊚ Griffin Lane ☎ 01603 701701 🌐 www.cityboats.co.uk

ⓔ enquiries@cityboats.co.uk) offers a range of trips leaving from various quays throughout the city.

If you need it, and hopefully you won't, the main **Police Station** is located on Bethel Street, close to The Forum.

ORIENTATION

Gentleman's Walk/Haymarket is the pedestrianised thoroughfare that runs through the city centre. Follow the side streets off here to discover more shops and cafés. Gentleman's Walk goes into **Exchange Street**, with **Gaol Hill** off to your left. **Jarrold** is nestled in the corner of Exchange Street and **London Street**. Continue for a few minutes down Exchange Street and then turn left on to **Lobster Lane** to discover the **Norwich Lanes**.

The **River Wensum** runs north and east of the main city centre. In the northeast corner you'll find the **cathedral** and **Cathedral Close**, beyond **Tombland**. Further out of the city is the railway station and **The Riverside** entertainment area, linked to the centre by **Prince of Wales Road**.

There are several boards displaying information and maps throughout the city, so it's difficult to get lost.

GETTING AROUND

Norwich is quite compact and much of the city centre is pedestrianised. The bus station is off Surrey Street and it has a café as well as a travel centre that provides timetables and travel information. It's not necessary to use public transport to get around the city centre. It's easier just to walk – but swap the heels for some comfy shoes, which will make the cobbled terrain much less hard on the feet.

By bike

Norwich is situated on National Route 1, which takes in the Marriott's Way – a disused railway line that runs the 22.5 km (14 miles) from Norwich to Reepham (where there's a train station and cycle hire). The outdoor shops in the city, Jarrold's book department and the library are good places to pick up maps. If you've brought your bike with you, then you'll be in good company – you'll find lots of people getting around on two wheels and there are plenty of places to park up in the city.

By bus

Areas around the city centre – near and far – are accessible by bus, and the bus is a good option for getting to those sights that sit a little outside the centre, such as the Sainsbury Centre for Visual Arts. Many buses leave from Norwich Bus Station, and others from the stands on St Stephen's Street and Castle Meadow. There's an information desk, plus timetables, at Norwich Bus Station, and staff who will help you plan your journey.

By taxi

If you want to get somewhere quickly, and without planning ahead, then there are several taxi ranks in the city with black cabs willing to take you to your destination. In the city centre, the best place to find a black cab is on Guildhall Hill (up the hill from Jarrold, just opposite Tesco Metro). Many of the local taxi companies have their offices on Prince of Wales Road – within stumbling distance of the pubs and clubs, but unless you're wanting a taxi on a Friday or Saturday night, then it's probably

◆ *Plentiful bike parking in St Gregory's Alley*

best to phone one of the following companies, rather than actually waiting in the offices:

1st Goldstar Taxis ☎ 01603 700700 ⓦ www.goldstartaxis.net
ABC Taxis ☎ 01603 666333 ⓦ http://abctaxisnorwich.co.uk
Beeline & Dolphin Taxis ☎ 01603 767676
Five Star ☎ 01603 455555 or 0800 575575
ⓦ www.5startaxis.com

Car hire

You can get to most places by bus or train but, if you'd prefer to explore the Norfolk coast and surrounding countryside on your own timetable, then hiring a car is a good option.

Norwich Car Hire @ Paddock Street, off Heigham Street
☎ 01603 666300 ⓦ www.norwichcarhire.co.uk
@ Norwich@norwichcarhire.co.uk
First Self Drive @ Paddock Street ☎ 01603 624275
ⓦ www.firstselfdrive.co.uk @ info@firstselfdrive.co.uk

▶ *Picture-perfect Pottergate*

THE CITY OF
Norwich

Introduction to city areas

Norwich is a small city, and that's part of its charm. Everything is within walking distance and the city centre blends seamlessly with Tombland, the area surrounding the cathedral and all the way down to Riverside. You'll easily flit between the two areas described in this book without even realising it.

For the purposes of this guide, the city is divided into two parts – the areas are separated along a north/south line marked by St Benedicts, Charing Cross, St Andrews, Bank Plain and Prince of Wales Road. The city centre area is everything south of this dividing line. The cathedral quarter and the river area are to the north of, and include, this dividing line.

The main landmark of the city centre is Norwich Castle and the cathedral provides a natural focal point for the second area. To walk between the two will take you less than ten minutes. Most of the sights and attractions are located in the city centre – as are most of the 'After Dark' options. The cathedral quarter and river offer a chance to escape from the hustle and bustle of the centre and are the perfect place to chill out and soak up some of the city's history and culture.

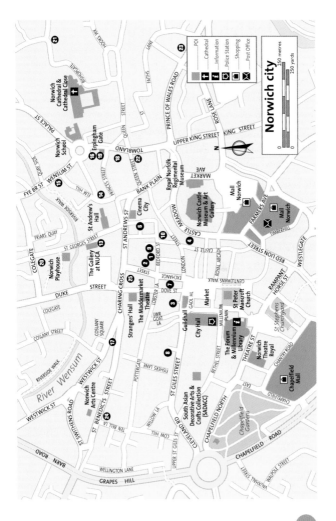

The city centre

The city centre itself is a hub of activity and home to an exhaustive selection of shops, including the Chapelfield shopping mall. There's also a healthy dollop of history too – in the form of the bold Norman castle. There are a couple of sights that sit just outside the city centre, but it's worth making the effort to visit the Cathedral of St John the Baptist, Dragon Hall and St Julian's Church & Shrine.

SIGHTS & ATTRACTIONS

Cathedral of St John the Baptist
Norwich is just one of a handful of cities that can boast two cathedrals – Norwich Cathedral (see pages 60–62) is Anglican and St John's, just outside the city centre, is its Roman Catholic counterpart. Dominated by the magnificent tower, which offers breathtaking views of the city, inside the cathedral is a grand open space characterised by fine detail – including some beautifully intricate stained glass. The cathedral is about a 10-minute walk from the city centre – head out of the city on Upper St Giles Street and take the pedestrian bridge over Grapes Hill to Earlham Road.
ⓐ Earlham Road ⓣ 01603 624615 ⓦ www.sjbcathedral.org.uk
ⓛ 07.30–19.30 daily ⓘ Charge for tower tours (book at tourist information centre for a guaranteed place)

Dragon Hall
Step back into Norwich's medieval past with a trip to the Grade-I-listed Dragon Hall. The hall was built by Robert Toppes and,

🔺 *The beautifully restored Dragon Hall*

today, it is Western Europe's only surviving trading hall built by one merchant. Inside, you can discover more about Robert Toppes and how he used the building, plus the way in which it has been utilised since. The Great Hall has been restored to its 15th-century state and is undoubtedly the most impressive part of the building. ⓐ 115–123 King Street ⓣ 01603 663922 ⓦ www.dragonhall.org ⏱ 10.00–16.00 Mon–Fri, 12.00–16.00 Sun & bank holidays, closed Sat (Mar–Nov); closed Dec–Mar except for special events

The Forum

The Norfolk and Norwich Millennium Library is the most visited in the country – and little wonder given its location. The striking glass-fronted building opened in 2001, seven years after the central library burnt down on the same site. But the futuristic city-centre construction is much more than a library. The building is also home to the tourist information centre, the local BBC, Café Bar Marzano on the ground floor, Pizza Express on the first floor and Fusion – Europe's largest permanent digital screen gallery. The ground floor plays host to markets,

⬤ *The magnificent Norman castle keep*

temporary art exhibitions and many other events, and the outside space is also utilised – at Christmas you'll find an ice rink and during the rest of the year there are a variety of other activities on offer. Perhaps more than anywhere else in the city, The Forum really represents what Norwich is all about – with the grandeur of St Peter Mancroft Church reflected in the glass frontage. It's worth grabbing a pizza just to stare out and admire the ecclesiastical view. ⓐ Millennium Plain, off Bethel Street ⓣ 01603 727950 ⓦ www.theforumnorwich.co.uk ⓣ 07.00–24.00 daily, closed Christmas Day & Boxing Day ⓘ Individual business hours vary

Norwich Castle Museum & Art Gallery

The box-shaped keep is what remains of Norwich's Norman castle. Originally a wooden motte-and-bailey castle built by William the Conqueror in 1067, the current structure, built on top of the motte, dates from 1120. Used as a prison for centuries, it has been a museum since 1894. Now it houses outstanding collections of fine art and archaeology, including vivid recreations of an Egyptian tomb and a tribute to local legend Boudica in the form of a ride on an Iceni warrior's chariot. The exhibits in the Natural History Gallery are bound to impress younger visitors and the Norfolk Wildlife section is good preparation for a visit to the coast and the rest of the county. The museum is also home to galleries displaying the work of the Norwich School of Artists. To get a real feel of the castle though, you'll need to head to the castle keep – the most architecturally impressive section of the museum. It's here that you'll get a sense of the castle and its place in the history of

Norwich and England. To explore the castle fully, book on a tour of the dungeons or battlements (separate charge for each). ⓐ Castle Meadow ⓣ 01603 493725 ⓦ www.museums. norfolk.gov.uk ⓔ museums@norfolk.gov.uk ⓛ 10.00–16.30 Mon–Sat, 13.00–16.30 Sun (Apr–late June & Oct–July); 10.00–17.00 Mon–Sat, 13.00–17.00 Sun (late June–Oct)

Plantation Garden

There's nothing from the road that hints at the existence of a beautiful Victorian garden just off it. Filled with all the grandeur and delicate detail of that period, the Plantation Garden is an oasis of calm, just a short walk from the centre – next to St John's Cathedral. The dell is surrounded by an elevated walkway, which allows you to appreciate fully the vision of Victorian businessman and keen gardener Henry Trevor. ⓐ 4 Earlham Road ⓣ 01603 621868 ⓦ www.plantationgarden.co.uk ⓛ 09.00–18.00 (or dusk if earlier) daily ❶ Admission charge

Royal Norfolk Regimental Museum

Leave the castle through the Natural History Gallery and follow signs to the Regimental Museum – you'll access it through a prison corridor and then a mock trench. The museum narrates the story of the Norfolk Regiment, from the Boer War right up to the current conflict in Afghanistan. As well as documenting the regiment's adventures abroad, it also reveals the daily life of a soldier. ⓐ Main entrance: Market Avenue, museum can also be accessed via the castle ⓣ 01603 493625 ⓦ www.museums.norfolk.gov.uk ⓛ 10.00–16.30 Tues–Sat, closed

🔺 *The shrine of Lady Julian*

Sun & Mon ❶ Admission charge (admission included in ticket to the castle)

St Julian's Church & Shrine

English mystic, Lady Julian of Norwich, was a hermit-like character who lived in the anchor hold at St Julian's Church in Norwich. Her famous visions were recorded in *The Revelations of Divine Love*, the first English book written by a woman. Mother Julian's shrine is in a room just off the small church – both are peaceful places for quiet contemplation away from the city centre. The Julian Centre, next door to the church, has a small gift- and bookshop plus further information on Lady Julian. ❹ Off Rouen Road, opposite the car park ❶ 01603 622509 ⓦ www.julianofnorwich.org ❶ Church and shrine: 07.30–16.30 daily; Julian Centre: 10.30–15.30 Mon–Sat, closed Sun

THE GOLDEN TRIANGLE

If you really want to embrace the local scene, then take a short walk out of the city and into 'the golden triangle'. The golden triangle seems to be ever expanding but, roughly, is considered to be the area between Earlham Road and Newmarket Road. Unthank Road goes straight through the middle of the golden triangle and the best pubs are just off it. It's a residential area and home to students, young professionals and families, with a variety of pubs and shops catering to their needs.
ⓦ www.goldentrianglenorwich.co.uk

CULTURE

The Maddermarket Theatre

Formerly a Catholic chapel, the medieval-looking Maddermarket is a suitably dramatic building that stages plays and performances in its intimate 300-seat auditorium. ⓐ St John's Alley ⓣ 01603 620917 ⓦ www.maddermarket.co.uk

Norwich Theatre Royal

The recent multi-million pound refurbishment of the Theatre Royal has transformed the building into an inviting and modern performance space. It hosts touring productions – from drama to comedy, musicals to dance – and, of course, the annual pantomime. Whether you're after a pre-theatre dinner or a pint of Adnams during the interval, there are several food and drink options available that will complete any evening. ⓐ Theatre Street ⓣ Box office: 01603 630000 ⓦ www.theatreroyalnorwich.co.uk

South Asian Decorative Arts & Crafts Collection (SADACC)

Housed in a beautiful old skating rink, just past the fire station on Bethel Street, SADACC can be found in the Country & Eastern building. It's a beautiful place in which to explore the artistic output of South Asia (and beyond). There are several cabinets, which host changing exhibitions, plus some more permanent fixtures. To appreciate fully all that's on offer, go upstairs and admire the parts of the collection that you can only see from the first floor (which is also the best place from which to admire the marvellous roof structure). The SADACC shares its home with Country & Eastern, so if the collection inspires you, you can take an exotic purchase back home – from reasonably priced cushion covers and mirrors to more substantial pieces of furniture. ⓐ Country & Eastern, The Old Skating Rink, 34–36 Bethel Street ⓣ 01603 663890 ⓦ www.southasian decorativeartsandcrafts.co.uk ⓛ 09.30–17.00 Mon–Fri, 09.30–17.30 Sat, closed Sun & bank holidays

● *Haymarket Square*

RETAIL THERAPY

For the ultimate retail therapy head straight for the Norwich Lanes, exploring the shops around Lobster Lane, Pottergate, Dove Street and Upper St Giles.

The Book Hive A recent addition to the city centre, The Book Hive is everything an independent bookshop should be. The interesting décor, charming children's area, on-hand expert knowledge, attentive service and the chance of a cuppa make this an ideal stop whatever your reading tastes. ❷ 53 London Street ❶ 01603 219268 ❿ www.thebookhive.co.uk ❶ 10.00–17.30 Mon, 09.30–17.30 Tues, Fri & Sat, 09.30–19.00 Thur

Catfish & Dogfish For an impressive selection of men and women's designer clothes head to Dogfish and, just down the street, its sister shop Catfish. From Vivienne Westwood to Diesel, there's plenty to choose from (or, depending on your cash flow, drool over). ❷ Dogfish: 6 Bedford Street ❶ 01603 762661 ❿ www.dogfishmen.co.uk ❶ 10.00–18.00 Mon–Sat, 11.00–16.30 Sun; ❷ Catfish: 24 Exchange Street ❶ 01603 619538 ❿ www.catfishwomen.com ❶ 10.00–18.00 Mon–Sat, 11.00–16.30 Sun

Chapelfield Chapelfield houses all the favourites including Superdry, French Connection, Mango, Zara and House of Fraser. If your shopping impulses aren't for clothes, though, there's an interactive Apple Store where you can play with all the latest gadgets. ❷ Entrances off St Stephens Street and Rampant Horse

Street **☎** 01603 753344 **Ⓦ** www.chapelfield.co.uk
🕐 09.00–18.00 Mon–Wed, 09.00–20.00 Thur, 09.00–19.00
Fri & Sat, 11.00–17.00 Sun (extended hours in the run-up
to Christmas)

Colman's Mustard Shop Enjoy a taste of Norwich back home
with a gift from the Colman's shop in the Royal Arcade. The
Victorian-style shop not only sells mustardy treats but also
narrates the history of this famous local brand. **ⓐ** 15 Royal
Arcade **☎** 01603 627889 **Ⓦ** www.mustardshopnorwich.co.uk
ⓔ info@mustardshopnorwich.co.uk **🕐** 09.30–17.00 Mon–Sat,
11.00–16.00 Sun (Apr–Dec)

Jarrold If you're in need of a department store while you're here,
then forget the usual high-street suspects and head for a
Norwich institution. There's an excellent cookware department
in the basement, a brilliant bookshop on the ground floor (the
place to go if you're interested in learning more about the area),
a well-stocked toy department, as well as a hairdressers, a MAC
make-up bar – plus all the usual homeware and fashion you'd
expect from a department store. It often hosts literary events
and book signings, so be sure to have a look on the website or in
the window to find out who's in town at the same time as you.
ⓐ 1–11 London Street **☎** 01603 660661 **Ⓦ** www.jarrold.co.uk
🕐 09.00–17.30 Mon, Wed & Fri, 09.30–17.30 Tues, 09.00–19.00
Thur, 09.00–18.00 Sat, 10.30–16.30 Sun

Poppy Valentine For vintage-inspired fashion head to Poppy
Valentine. Suitably located in the grand Royal Arcade, this

⬧ *Frank's Bar*

original and quirky outlet has set up home in Norwich, having moved from trendy Portobello Market. You'll find retro-looking dresses among the individual items on offer – every one made from original vintage fabric. ❸ Castle Street entrance to the Royal Arcade ❶ 01603 928802 ⓦ www.poppyvalentine.com ⓔ info@poppyvalentine.com ⓛ 09.30–17.30 Mon–Sat, closed Sun

TAKING A BREAK

Frank's Bar £ ❶ For a friendly welcome and a perfect place to chill out and recharge, head to Frank's Bar. The lunch menu offers something a bit different from the usual sandwiches and paninis and, on a cold day, a mug of chai latte takes some beating. If you're there later in the day when the evening menus come out, you might end up staying for longer than you'd

anticipated. ⓐ 19 Bedford Street ⓣ 01603 618902 ⓛ 10.30–24.00
Tues–Thur, 10.30–02.30 Fri & Sat, 10.30–23.30 Sun, closed Mon

No. 33 £ ❷ If you're after some lunch or an afternoon tea and
cake, there's nowhere better – which is probably why No. 33 is
always busy. Don't go starving as you may have to hang around
for a table, but the posh mushrooms on toast are worth waiting
for. And that's before you even get started on the cakes.
ⓐ 33 Exchange Street ⓣ 01603 626097 ⓛ 08.00–17.30 Mon–Fri,
09.30–17.30 Sat, 10.30–16.30 Sun

Pulse Café Bar £ ❸ You'll find Pulse tucked away in a courtyard
off Guildhall Hill. Serving delicious vegetarian food, it's a great
stop for lunch (although it can get busy) and will open the
eyes of even meat-craving carnivores. Interesting food served
in a great setting. ⓐ The Old Fire Station Stables, Labour in
Vain Yard ⓣ 01603 765562 ⓦ http://pulsecafébar.co.uk
ⓛ 10.00–17.00 Mon & Tues, 10.00–20.00 Wed–Sat,
11.30–16.00 Sun

Thai Si Paak £ ❹ If you want to grab a quick and tasty lunch
that will keep you going through an afternoon of sightseeing
and shopping, choose one of the curries on offer at Thai Si Paak.
It's not ideal for a lingering lunch but if you want a tasty Thai
curry and you want one now, this is the place. If you would
prefer your Thai in a more glamorous setting, then the owners
also run Baan Phraya on Red Lion Street. ⓐ 7 Castle Street
ⓣ 01603 632641 ⓦ www.thaisipaak.com ⓔ eat@thaisipaak.com
ⓛ 11.00–18.00 Mon–Sat, 11.00–16.00 Sun

Baby Buddha Chinese Teahouse ££ ❺ The Baby Buddha is a
local favourite for those in search of delicious Cantonese cuisine
and the teahouse's speciality, dim sum. ⓐ 139 Ber Street
❶ 01603 490889 ⓦ www.babybuddha-teahouse.co.uk
ⓔ info@babybuddha-teahouse.co.uk ⓛ 12.00–22.00 Thur–Tues,
closed Wed

Bishop's ££ ❻ If you want to treat yourself to a special lunch,
then find your way to Bishop's, tucked away down St Andrews
Hill. The two- or three-course lunch special (complete with

⬥ *London Street*

glass of wine) makes for an indulgent lunchtime treat or, if you're looking for something a little later in the day, head here in the evening – for full-blown fine dining or just a glass of wine. ⓐ 8–10 St Andrews Hill ⓣ 01603 767321 ⓦ www.bishopsrestaurant.co.uk ⓔ reservations@ bishopsrestaurant.co.uk ⓛ 12.00–14.30, 18.00–21.45 (wine bar open from 17.00) Tues–Sat, closed Sun & Mon

The Vine ££ ❼ In this pub-cum-restaurant you can have good food *and* good beer. Downstairs is a pub and upstairs an intimate dining area where you can wash down delicious Thai food with a pint of real ale. The beer has been selected to complement the food, and the landlady will happily suggest something to go with your dinner. The Vine makes for a unique dining experience but be sure to book – the 'intimate' dining space really is quite intimate! ⓐ Dove Street ⓣ 01603 627362 ⓛ 12.00–15.00, 17.00–23.00 daily

The Waffle House ££ ❽ For something a bit different, The Waffle House offers a selection of sweet and savoury waffles with a range of tempting toppings – and some real treats on the specials board. ⓐ 39 St Giles Street ⓣ 01603 612790 ⓦ www.wafflehouse.co.uk/ norwich ⓛ 10.00–22.00 Mon–Sat, 11.00–22.00 Sun

AFTER DARK

Bedfords ❾ Just up the cobbled street from Karma Kafé is Bedfords, housed in a beautiful old building complete with crypt. It's a great place to chill out with friends over a few drinks or, if you're feeling peckish, there's a tempting menu to draw you in too. ⓐ 1 Old Post Office Yard, off Bedford Street ⓣ 01603 666869 ⓛ 11.30–15.00 Mon, 11.30–15.00, 17.00–23.00 Tues–Thur, 11.30–15.00, 17.00–01.00 Fri, 11.30–01.00 Sat, closed Sun (except before a bank holiday)

Karma Kafé ⓰ A good compromise between a city-centre bar and the clubs of Prince of Wales Road, you can dance the night away at Karma Kafé. From the vault to the terrace bar, there are three floors to make your way through – not to mention the list of wines and cocktails. ⓐ 18 Bedford Street ⓦ www.mykarmakafe.com ⓔ info@mykarmakafe.com

Riverside ⓱ The Riverside Leisure Complex can be found opposite the train station. If you're coming from the city, turn right after the bridge at the bottom of Prince of Wales Road. As well as a cinema, there's a selection of chain restaurants, some bars, a bowling alley and a club. If you're after a night out, it's a good place to come, although, for a greater variety of establishments, the city-centre options come with more atmosphere and individuality. ⓐ Off Koblenz Avenue ⓦ www.riversidenorwich.co.uk

The Waterfront ⓲ If the chain-offerings of Riverside leave you desiring something a little different, The Waterfront is just over the river and can be accessed by the footbridge from Riverside. The indie venue hosts live music and regular club nights on a Friday and Saturday. ⓐ 139–141 King Street ⓣ 01603 632717 ⓦ www.waterfrontnorwich.com ⓔ info@waterfrontnorwich.com

The cathedral quarter & the river

On the outskirts of the city centre proper sits Norwich's iconic cathedral, situated in its peaceful and beautiful close – offering a sense of calm in an otherwise bustling city. Elm Hill is just around the corner to complete the historical offering and, as night falls, there are enough pubs and cultural treats to keep you in this part of the city well past bedtime.

SIGHTS & ATTRACTIONS

Elm Hill
The beautiful cobbled street that runs from Princes Street to Wensum Street is the most historic in Norwich – and you'll soon see why. Flanked by Tudor buildings – there are more in Elm Hill than in the whole of the city of London – it's a step back in time and is an historical artefact as well as a film set (used in Hollywood blockbuster *Stardust*). The river can be accessed by Elm Hill Quay, to your left as you walk down towards Wensum Street. It's a quiet and pretty place from which to admire the river. You can stop for tea and coffee at the top (Briton's Arms) and at the bottom (Olive's).

Norwich Cathedral & Cathedral Close
The Cathedral Close envelops the stunning cathedral and is a special place in which to escape the hurry and scurry of the city centre. At 18 hectares (44 acres), it is one of the largest in the country and home to listed buildings, the Norwich School and, of course, the stunning Norman cathedral. Off Tombland, a little

● *Historic Elm Hill*

outside today's city centre, Norwich Cathedral is an iconic image of the city. You can catch glimpses of it from several vantage points as you arrive into Norwich and its impressive spire dominates the city skyline.

The foundation stone was laid in 1096 and, more than 900 years on, the cathedral is a bustling and welcoming place today – despite its long and often troubled past. The cloister is perhaps the most obvious reminder of the Benedictine priory that once occupied the site and is the largest of its kind in the country. Walking around it will give you a sense of life in the cathedral as it once was. The newly built Hostry and Refectory cleverly symbolise the cathedral today – a fusion of old and new. You will enter the cathedral through the Hostry (except on Sundays) – to the right of the main cathedral entrance as you come into the close through the Erpingham Gate.

⬥ *The Cloisters at Norwich Cathedral*

EDITH CAVELL

Just alongside the Erpingham Gate, outside the cathedral, is a memorial to Norwich's famous daughter, Edith Cavell. Born in Swardeston, just a few miles out of the city, Edith Cavell left her Norfolk home for Brussels, first as a governess and later as a nurse. It was while serving as a nurse during World War I that she helped hundreds of troops – both Allied and German – escape from Belgium. She paid with her life when, in 1915, she was executed. Her body was returned to Norwich Cathedral and today, almost 100 years after her death, a graveside service is still held every year, and the memorial outside the cathedral is a permanent reminder of the sacrifice she made.

The Refectory is housed in an award-winning building and is the perfect spot to refuel and take in the magnificence of this very special place. Just around the corner from the refectory, in the Cathedral Close, is a small herb garden (🕐 09.00–17.00 daily). 🕿 01603 218300 🅦 www.cathedral.org.uk 🕐 07.30–18.00 daily; tours: 11.00, 12.00, 13.00, 14.00, 15.00 Mon–Sat ❶ No charge for entrance or tours, donations appreciated

River Wensum & Cow Tower

Cow Tower stands on the River Wensum as it winds its way out of the city. Built at the close of the 14th century, Cow Tower once formed part of the city's defences and has played an important role in the history of the city ever since. It was a victim of Kett's Rebellion and was set on fire by Kett's followers as they tried to enter the city. Unfortunately for Kett's men, some of them would return to Cow Tower on their departure from the city and from this life.

Pulls Ferry, slightly further along the river, is an idyllic spot and one without such a bloody history. The beautiful arched building was once the gateway to a canal, which led to the cathedral and was used to transport the stone that would help build it. On a fine day, a riverside walk is a lovely way to explore the city. Starting at the Adam and Eve pub (see page 73) you'll easily be able to trace yourself a route along the river. Visit Norwich has also detailed a specific riverside walk, which can be downloaded here: ⓦ http://www.visitnorwich.co.uk/documents/310.pdf

🔺 *A riverside walk is an ideal way to see the city*

Strangers' Hall

Continuing the historical theme of this part of Norwich, Strangers' Hall chronicles Tudor to Victorian history in the beautiful setting of a medieval town house. Rich in domestic artefacts, the collections here tell the stories of those who have called Strangers' Hall home and reveal fascinating details of life in Norwich, and in England, at that time. ⓐ Charing Cross ⓣ 01603 667229 ⓦ www.museums.norfolk.gov.uk ⓛ 10.30–16.00 Wed–Sat, closed Mon, Tues & Sun (Mar–Dec); closed Jan & Feb ⓘ Admission charge

CULTURE

Cinema City

Alongside current films, Cinema City also screens classic and forgotten movies, plus National Theatre and Met Opera performances and has regular Q&As with film directors. You can enjoy a drink in the bar before and after the performance and, even better, take your drink into the screen with you. The Dining Rooms completes the offering with pre- and post-performance meals and a delicious menu. You don't even have to see a film. ⓐ St Andrew's Street ⓣ Box office: 0871 902 5724; The Dining Rooms: 07504 356378 ⓦ www.picturehouses.co.uk/cinema/Cinema_City

The Gallery at Norwich University College of the Arts (NUCA)

The Gallery hosts temporary exhibitions not only of NUCA students but also artists from across the country and around the globe. The programme is always changing but, whatever is on, you can trust it will be unusual, contemporary and boundary-pushing. ⓐ St Georges Street ⓣ 01603 756247 ⓦ www.nuca.ac.uk/the-gallery-at-nuca ⓔ gallery@nuca.ac.uk ⓛ 10.00–17.00 Mon–Sat, closed Sun (opening hours vary for individual exhibitions, so check the website ahead of visiting)

The King of Hearts

Culture is alive and kicking on the banks of the River Wensum where this Tudor building houses a café, art gallery, gift shop and music room all under one roof. It hosts recitals, concerts, storytelling and art exhibitions. The future of the King of Hearts is currently uncertain. It's likely that the café will remain but how the rest of the building will be used is presently unknown. ⓐ 7–15 Fye Bridge Street, between Wensum and Magdalen Street ⓣ 01603 766129 ⓦ www.kingofhearts.org.uk

Norwich Arts Centre

The Arts Centre is probably the best place in the city to listen to live music on account of its excellent acoustics – thanks to the fact that it used to be a church. Alongside performances, the centre hosts exhibitions and runs courses on such subjects as photography and creative writing. ⓐ St Benedicts ⓣ Box office: 01603 660352 ⓦ www.norwichartscentre.co.uk

Norwich Ghost Walks

It's little wonder that a city with such a long and interesting history has a few ghosts in its closet, and the Man in Black is the one who lets them out. Revealing local tales of ghostliness, witchery, murders and cannibalism, the walks not only provide great entertainment but they are also a good way to see the city and learn a bit of its history. Walks leave from the Adam and Eve pub (see page 73) at 19.30 on Monday, Tuesday and Thursday evenings from January to November, and on Thursdays only in December. There's no need to book, just turn up on the night – you'll soon identify your host. ❶ 07831 189985 ⓦ www. ghostwalksnorwich.co.uk ⓔ norwichmaninblack@yahoo.co.uk

Norwich Playhouse

The Playhouse is a friendly and low-key venue welcoming stand-up comedians, touring plays and a range of drama and music performances. It is also home to the Playhouse Bar, which is a great place to enjoy a drink by day and by night (when there are often DJs at the weekends), whether or not there's a performance on. ⓐ St Georges Street ❶ Box office: 01603 598598; bar: 01603 766669 ⓦ www.norwichplayhouse.org.uk ⓔ info@norwichplayhouse.co.uk ⓑ Bar: 10.00–24.00 Mon–Sat, 12.00–24.00 Sun

RETAIL THERAPY

Elm Hill Olde-worlde shops line either side of Elm Hill, as is fitting in this picturesque old street. There are several antiques shops but also a games shop, bookshop and a couple of crafts shops. The Jade Tree has a beautiful collection of gifts, and there's a workshop and gallery that you can access through a door from the shop. Elm Hill Crafts Shop also has some lovely pieces on display – for babies, children and adults.

The Bear Shop on Elm Hill probably deserves a special mention. It's jam-packed with bears of all shapes and sizes. Whether you're young or old, if you're into all things furry, prepare to fall in love. ⓐ 18 Elm Hill ① 01603 766866 ⓦ www.bearshops.co.uk ① 10.00– 17.00 Mon– Fri, 09.30– 17.00 Sat, open Sun by appointment: call to make arrangements

Prim Full of wearable vintage fashion for men and women, this welcoming boutique is situated on St Benedicts Street. For unique clothing and accessories for him and her, it's the perfect stop for a bit of individuality. ⓐ 14 St Benedicts ① 01603 766261 ⓦ www.primvintagefashion.com ① 10.00–18.00 Mon–Sat, closed Sun

TAKING A BREAK

Amaretto £ ⓭ If you're not already hungry, the window display and specials board will soon give you an appetite. There's a well-stocked deli along with daily specials and tempting cakes to take away. It's the perfect stop for picnic fodder and if you continue down St Georges Street towards the river, then you'll arrive at St Georges Green – the ideal spot for some alfresco dining. ⓐ 16 St Georges Street ① 01603 767478 ⓦ www.amarettodeli.co.uk ⓔ amarettodeli@yahoo.co.uk ① 08.00–17.30 Mon & Tues, 08.00–18.00 Wed–Sat, closed Sun

Britons Arms £ ⓮ Situated at the top of Elm Hill, the Britons Arms provides a well-located coffee stop. The perfect place for a tea and cake, or something a bit more substantial, the

⬥ *Norwich Playhouse – a welcoming venue for a wet night*

charming thatched-roof coffee house is as lovely on the inside as it is on the out – with a roaring fire to warm you up on colder days. ⓐ 9 Elm Hill ⓣ 01603 623397 ⓛ 09.30–17.00 Mon–Sat, closed Sun

Olive's £ ⓯ If you're up early, kick-start a day of sightseeing with breakfast at Olive's. Or, if you're a late riser, there's a delicious selection of toasties and sandwiches available at lunchtime. There's also a good drinks menu – whether you're after something soft or strong, hot or cold. And, just round the corner from the cathedral and at the foot of Elm Hill, it's also in a pretty unbeatable location. ⓐ 40 Elm Hill ⓣ 01603 230500 ⓦ www.olivesnorwich.co.uk ⓛ 08.00–16.00 Mon–Thur, 08.00–23.00 Fri, 09.00–23.00 Sat, 10.00–15.00 Sun

Take 5 £ ⓰ Whether you're after a delicious helping of home-made cake, a tasty lunch or dinner, or a pint of ale, you'll find it all at Take 5, along with a laid-back atmosphere – and all in a beautiful old building. The downstairs crypt is a bit special – try to sneak a peek or, even better, listen to some live music there if something's on. ⓐ 17 Tombland ⓣ 01603 614210 ⓛ 11.00–late Mon–Sat, open Sundays in winter only

Pinocchios ££ ⓱ For good Italian food in a laid-back atmosphere, Pinocchios serves up tasty pasta dishes and pizzas, plus an à la carte menu if you need more choice. The lunchtime and early-bird deals are good value. For added atmosphere, visit on one of the live-music nights.

ⓐ 11 St Benedicts ⓣ 01603 613318 ⓦ www.pinocchios
restaurant.net ⓛ 17.00–23.00 Mon, 12.00–14.00, 17.00–23.00
Tues–Fri, 12.00–23.00 Sat, closed Sun

Shiki Japanese Restaurant ££ ⓲ For tasty Japanese food – from
either the main menu, sushi menu or Teppanyaki menu – Shiki
is a good choice, located in the heart of the city's after-dark
action. If you can't decide what you want, then opt for one of
the delicious bento boxes. ⓐ 6 Tombland ⓣ 01603 619262
ⓦ www.shikirestaurant.co.uk ⓔ bookings@shikirestaurant.co.uk
ⓛ 12.00–14.30, 17.30–23.00 Mon–Sat, closed Sun

Trattoria Rustica ££ ⓳ This cosy restaurant tucked just behind
Tombland on the cobbled Princes Street is full of character, and
serves tasty Italian dishes. Well located and with all your Italian
favourites on the menu. ⓐ 20 Princes Street ⓣ 01603 621043
ⓦ www.trattoriarustica.com ⓛ 18.00–24.00 Mon–Sat; also
18.00–22.00 Sun (Easter–summer only)

Last Wine Bar ££–£££ ⓴ If you're after something a bit special,
then the Last Wine Bar is a good choice for a luxury lunch or an
evening-time treat. The tempting specials menu will draw you in
and, once you're there, there's an extensive wine list and delicious
menu to keep you seated all night. To enjoy a relaxed atmosphere
and some of the historical detail of the building, opt to sit in the
bar and, if the pennies won't stretch to a full dinner, there's a
good-value bar menu from which to choose. ⓐ St Georges Street
ⓣ 01603 626626 ⓦ www.lastwinebar.co.uk ⓛ 12.00–14.30, 17.00–
00.30 Mon–Fri, 12.00–14.30, 18.00–00.30 Sat, closed Sun

⬥ *Cow Tower on the banks of the Wensum*

AFTER DARK

Adam and Eve ㉑ Drinkers have been frequenting this pub for centuries; it's Norwich's oldest and worth a visit for historical, if not alcoholic, reasons. It's warm, friendly and, as you'd expect from a pub that's been serving ale since the 13th century, cosy and traditional. ⓐ Bishopgate ⓣ 01603 667423 ⓦ www.adamandevenorwich.co.uk ⓛ 11.00–23.00 Mon–Sat, 12.00–22.30 Sun

Beluga ㉒ If you've had your share of real ale and traditional pubs, then head to Beluga for something a bit more refined. The baroque detail and ornate touches add a bit of glamour and the cocktails will make a refreshing change from beer. ⓐ 2 Upper King Street, off Tombland ⓦ www.mybeluga.co.uk ⓔ info@mybeluga.co.uk ⓛ 11.30–24.00 Tues–Thur, 11.30–01.30 Fri & Sat, closed Sun & Mon

Mercy ㉓ If you're after some serious clubbing, then Mercy, towards the bottom of Prince of Wales Road, is where you'll be heading – it's the city's biggest club. ⓐ Prince of Wales Road ⓣ 01603 626300 ⓦ www.mercynightclub.com ⓔ info@mercynightclub.com

The Plough ㉔ The beer at the Plough comes from the Grain Brewery just down the road and the ingredients for that beer come from East Anglia, making it a great place to head for a real taste of local life. As well as good drink, there's a lovely beer garden, which just about manages to contain the thirsty hordes

who come here on a summer evening. 🅐 58 St Benedicts Street
🅣 01603 661384 🅔 info@theploughnorwich.co.uk 🅛 12.00–23.00
Sun–Thur, 12.00–24.00 Fri & Sat

Rumsey Wells 🈺 The Rumsey Wells manages to combine
comfort with style, mixed together with a great atmosphere –
whether you've come for an early evening drink, an afternoon
of beer and board-game revelry (there's a selection of games
to choose from) or a proper night out. There's also a menu
to tempt you to stay a bit longer. 🅐 4 St Andrews Street
🅣 01603 614858

▶ *A view over the marshes at Blakeney*

OUT OF TOWN

trips

The Norfolk coast

The Norfolk coast stretches from The Wash in the west round to the Suffolk border, just north of Lowestoft. In between is a beautiful coastline characterised by long sandy beaches, charming towns and villages, and unspoilt countryside. Erosion is fast changing the face of the Norfolk coastline and, if you need some convincing of climate change, places like Happisburgh are a beautiful but sad reminder that it is very much a reality.

The long stretch of coast is a diverse landscape – there are posh towns (Holt and Burnham Market), seaside towns (Hunstanton and Cromer), long, deep sandy expanses of beach (at Wells and Holkham) and more pebbly versions (at Sheringham).

Beyond the kitsch seaside image of Great Yarmouth, the Norfolk coast has much to offer. Follow its entire length and, alongside the places listed here, you'll discover some quiet and unspoilt beaches of your own.

GETTING THERE

If you're coming from the city, the main road heading east is the A47 and you'll leave this at different points depending upon your coastal destination. For north Norfolk, follow the A140 out of the city towards Cromer. If you're heading west, then the A1067 towards Fakenham will send you in the direction of Brancaster. The A149 follows the coast, so if you're not sure where to head, then follow this and stop off along the way to explore.

THE PEDDARS WAY

The Peddars Way runs 150 km (93 miles) from Holme-next-the-Sea to Knettishall in Suffolk, tracing the route of an old Roman road. If you don't fancy the almost 160-km (100-mile) walk, you can easily do shorter sections of it and, using the local bus service, you won't need to go back on yourself. If you'd prefer to traverse the route on bike or horse, it's possible on some sections. For more information, visit ⓦ www.nationaltrail.co.uk/PeddarsWay and ⓦ www.peddarsway.com

Trains leave from Norwich station for Sheringham and Great Yarmouth (with stops along the way). You can also get a bus to most coastal destinations – First Buses leave Norwich Bus Station for Lowestoft and Great Yarmouth, and Sanders Coaches (ⓣ 01263 712800 ⓦ www.sanderscoaches.com ⓔ info@sanderscoaches.com ⓦ www.travelineastanglia.co.uk for timetable information) go from Castle Meadow to Wells-next-the-Sea, Blakeney, Holt, Sheringham, Cromer, Mundesley, Caister and Great Yarmouth. Visit the information centre at Norwich Bus Station for up-to-date information on routes, times and destinations.

SIGHTS & ATTRACTIONS

Blakeney

The landscape at Blakeney has inspired artists and it's easy to see why. It is very different from the sandy beaches to the

west and particularly enchanting on a winter's day, when you can hear the stays jangling against the boat masts beyond the quay. Leaving the car park, you can walk towards Blakeney spit and the salt marshes – the route takes you all the way round to Cley where you can stop for refreshments before heading back to Blakeney. To visit the seals of Blakeney Point, you'll need to catch one of the boat trips leaving from Morston Quay. Companies including Beans (ⓦ www.beansboattrips.co.uk) and Temples (ⓦ www.sealtrips.co.uk) run regular trips to see the seals from here.

Brancaster & the Burnhams

The long and sandy beach at Brancaster is a favourite of windsurfers and kite-boarders when the wind is blowing in the right direction. Pick up something fishy at the Crab Hut or, if it's the season, many of the houses will be selling bags of mussels – just pop your money in the box.

Heading east out of Brancaster, towards the Staithe, you'll begin to come across the Burnhams. Just past the Staithe is the flourishing fishing and sailing community of Burnham Deepdale. A few miles further inland is Burnham Market – the biggest of the Burnhams. The road going through Burnham Market is flanked by deep green lawns and, beyond these, a selection of shops, galleries and eateries.

Moving eastwards, Burnham Overy is the next of the Burnhams. At Burnham Overy Staithe, you can park up at the front and walk along the creek to the beach. Take a picnic and some comfy shoes and spend a day there tucked up in the dunes.

Cromer

The expansive beaches of Holkham and Wells make way for the seaside towns of Cromer and Sheringham. Perched on a clifftop, Cromer is the natural place to pick up a local delicacy – the Cromer crab. Enjoy yours, or some fish and chips, on the sandy beach or the pier. At the bottom of the pier you'll find the lifeboat station – it's well worth a visit and serves as a reminder that the coastline here can be dangerous as well as beautiful. The maritime theme continues at the Henry Blogg Lifeboat Museum and the Cromer Museum. **RNLI Henry Blogg Lifeboat Museum** ⓐ The Rocket House, The Gangway ⓣ 01263 511294 ⓛ 10.00–16.00 Tues–Sun, closed Mon (open until 17.00 Apr–Sept), open weekends only in December, closed in January; **Cromer Museum** ⓐ Tucker Street ⓣ 01263 513543 ⓦ www.museums.norfolk.gov.uk ⓛ 10.00–17.00 Mon–Sat,

⬤ *Big skies over Cromer beach*

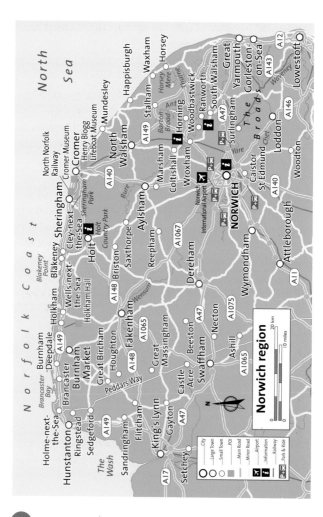

13.00–16.00 Sun (Mar–Oct); 10.00–16.00 Mon–Sat, closed Sun (Nov–Feb) ❶ Admission charge

Holkham

Holkham Hall sits in a beautiful 1,200-hectare (3,000-acre) setting. Hundreds of deer call the park home, as does the Coke family, who live at the hall. Step back in time at the Bygones Museum, or, for a taste of aristocratic life, visit the hall. But you don't need to go inside to enjoy the beautiful setting of Holkham Hall – there are several walks around the extensive grounds, plus the newly opened walled gardens. The beach at Holkham is just across the road, through the car park. Backed by a pine forest, the beautiful expanse of sand has been used as a film set (*Shakespeare in Love*) and it's easy to see why – it really is a romantic spot. **Holkham Hall** ⓦ www.holkham.co.uk ⏱ Hall: 12.00–16.00 Mon, Thur & Sun, closed Tues, Wed, Fri & Sat (Apr–Oct only); **Bygones Museum and History of Farming Exhibition**: ⏱ 10.00–17.00 daily (Apr–Oct); park: 07.00–19.00 Mon–Sat, 09.00–19.00 Sun (Apr–Oct); 07.00–19.00 Mon, Wed, Fri & Sat, 09.30–19.00 Tues & Thur; 09.00–19.00 Sun (Nov–Mar); walled gardens: 12.00–16.00 daily (Apr–Oct) ❶ Admission charge for Hall and museums, redeemable parking charge for car park

Holt

It's not strictly on the coast, but it would be a real shame not to visit Holt as you explore this part of the county. A perfect blend of town and country, Holt is home to some wonderful independent shops, cafés and pubs. The best place for some retail therapy on the coast.

Sheringham

The pebbled beach at Sheringham gives way to sand as you walk eastwards along the promenade. The pretty seaside town has a couple of pubs, some cafés and a few crafty-type shops. The countryside isn't far away either – Sheringham Park has signposted walks and is particularly stunning when the rhododendrons are in full bloom. Sheringham is also home to the North Norfolk Railway and, as you walk through the park, you are bound to see, or hear, a steam train puffing its way along the coast. Departing from Sheringham, the train makes the 16-km (10-mile) journey towards Holt, and a rover ticket will allow you to fully explore all the towns and stations on the way. **Sheringham Park** ⓐ Wood Farm, Upper Sheringham ⓣ 01263 820550 ⓛ Park: all year ⓘ Car park charge for non-National Trust members; **North Norfolk Railway** ⓣ 01263 820800; timetable: 01263 820800 ⓦ www.nnrailway.co.uk

Wells-next-the-Sea

The beach at Wells is very similar to that at Holkham – with great expanses of sand and dunes in which to hide if it gets particularly blustery. Similarly, the beach is backed by pine forest, but the colourful beach huts add a more seaside-like feel – as do the fish and chip and rock shops in town. It's a beautiful spot on the Norfolk coast, but be careful if you plan to swim – the tides can be dangerous if you're not familiar with the area.

TAKING A BREAK

Picnic Fayre £ For the tastiest, poshest picnic, head to the Picnic Fayre at Cley for your supplies. From mouth-watering

🔺 *Beach huts facing out to sea at Wells*

savouries to delicious sweet treats, the deli serves up fresh produce and much, much more. Get there hungry.
🅐 The Old Forge, Cley 📞 01263 740587 🅦 www.picnic-fayre.co.uk
🕐 09.00–17.00 Mon–Sat, 10.00–16.00 Sun

Cookies Crab Shop £–££ Cookies serves fresh, tasty seafood in a summer house and makeshift outdoor dining space. Their royal salads really are something special. 🅐 The Green at Salthouse
📞 01263 740352 🕐 Winter: 10.00–16.00 daily; rest of the year: 09.00–19.00 daily ❗ Booking advisable, especially at weekends

Byfords £–£££ A café, restaurant, deli and posh B&B all in a beamed building just off the High Street, Byfords is a Holt institution. The perfect stop for a delicious slice of cake or something more substantial. 🅐 1–3 Shirehall Plain
📞 01263 711400 🅦 www.byfords.org.uk

The Broads

The Norfolk Broads are a unique watery landscape, the country's largest protected wetland. They consist of around 200 km (124 miles) of lock-free waterways, nestled in between Norwich and the coastline. At places like Horsey Mill, Norfolk's famously flat landscape offers spectacular views across the Broads.

The Broads are not a natural phenomenon, as once thought. They are the result of peat excavation, which started in the Middle Ages and, over time, flooded the land here until it represented the unique wetland we now see. Today, this remarkable man-made landscape is a holiday destination and recreation space for both locals and visitors alike. The Broads vary in size and feel, and are linked together by six rivers – the Ant, Thurne, Bure, Yare, Chet and Waveney. You can explore the Broads close to the city centre or out towards the coast – you won't need to go far. The River Yare, as it goes through Bramerton and Surlingham, is particularly lovely before it opens up at Rockland Broad – and there are a few good pubs en route.

GETTING THERE

You'll have to head east for your Broads adventure. If driving, the A47 or A146 will start you in the right direction. Or, if you're heading to Wroxham, take the Wroxham Road (A1151) out of the city. First buses go out to Loddon and Wroxham, and Anglian buses service Surlingham and Rockland.

SIGHTS & ATTRACTIONS

Horsey

If you don't have much time to explore the county, then head to Horsey, where you can experience the Norfolk coast at its sandy best (complete with seal pups on the shore in the winter months) and the picturesque Broads – each just a few miles from one another. The windpump at Horsey provides an iconic image of the broadland landscape as it looks across the flat fields towards the sea. There's a lovely walk that takes you from the car park across the fields and along the river round to the thatched church and village. Conveniently, you can also detour to the Nelson Head (ⓐ The Street ⓣ 01493 393378 ⓦ www.nelsonheadhorsey.co.uk) for some refreshments.

The beach at Horsey is accessed by a gravel track – the quality of which varies throughout the year. You can, however, park at the top and walk down to the beach. During the winter months, follow the path behind the dunes to a specifically constructed viewing platform where you can see seal pups and their mothers on the beach. Horsey Mere ⓐ off the B1159 ⓘ Admission charge for Horsey Windpump; car park charges

Ranworth & South Walsham

Ranworth is a beautiful, laid-back Norfolk village and the perfect place in which to experience the Norfolk Broads. When you park up, you actually have Malthouse Broad in front of you, rather confusingly, and not Ranworth Broad. A boardwalk will take you out of the car park and to the visitor centre on Ranworth Broad. For spectacular views across the Broads, make your way to St Helen's Church and climb the winding staircase to the top of the tower. The church even has a teashop nearby if you need a hot drink after your heady ascent. ● Nature reserve: dawn till dusk, daily; visitor centre: 10.00–17.00 daily (Apr–Oct)

South Walsham is just a couple of miles from Ranworth (and it makes a lovely walk). For a cultivated experience of the Broads, head to Fairhaven Woodland and Water Garden, just off the A47, before you reach Ranworth, which is a pretty spot – particularly special when the woodland is in full bloom.

ⓐ South Walsham, follow the signs from the A47 ❶ 01603 270449 ⓦ www.fairhavengarden.co.uk ● 10.00–17.00 daily (Mar–Nov); 10.00–16.00 daily (Dec–Feb)

Wroxham

Wroxham is the broadland equivalent of the seaside towns on the coast. It can be a bit tacky but it's nevertheless a good place to see the River Bure, have a drink by the water's edge and admire the waterside dwellings (the King's Head is a good spot

TAKING TO THE WATER

The best way to see the Broads is on them. Boats can be hired from Wroxham or, to get even closer to the water, explore the waterways with a canoe. **The Canoe Man** (ⓦ www.thecanoeman.com) offers guided canoe trips around the county, and canoes can also be hired independently from **Martham Boats** (❶ 01493 740249 ⓦ www.marthamboats.com).

for exactly that). For a bit of retail therapy, head to Wroxham Barns. There are shops selling arts, crafts, clothes and green-fingered treats, a farmers' market on the second Saturday of the month and a junior farm to keep the kids happy. ❷ Tunstead Road, Hoveton ❶ 01603 783762 ⓦ www.wroxham-barns.co.uk ⓛ 10.00–17.00 daily; junior farm may have restricted opening hours, especially in winter, so phone ahead ❶ Admission charge for junior farm

TAKING A BREAK

Staithe 'N' Willow £ Whether you want to stop for breakfast, baguettes, afternoon tea or something more substantial, the Staithe 'N' Willow is a traditional, thatch-roofed tearoom. When the weather's fine, the garden is a great place to relax in and, if you really like the laid-back vibe in this broadland village, the Staithe 'N' Willow also has a holiday cottage for hire. ❷ 16 Lower Street, Horning ❶ 01692 630915 ⓦ http://broads-norfolk.co.uk/Staithe-Willow

Coldham Hall Tavern ££ For sweeping views across the Broads, head to this recently refurbished pub, hidden away on the Broads at Surlingham – about 10 km (6 miles) southeast of the city. Good food is served in the smart new dining area. ❷ Surlingham ❶ 01508 538366 ⓦ www.coldhamhalltavern.co.uk ⓛ Food: 12.00–14.00, 18.00–21.00 Mon–Sat, 12.00–15.00 Sun

The Fur and Feather Inn ££ The beer here has even made it into some of the food at this lovely pub on the river at Woodbastwick

– also home of Woodforde's Brewery. There's an extensive menu to choose from and a selection of ales, straight from the barrel, behind the bar. If you're taking your drinking seriously, then join a brewery tour (ⓦ www.woodfordes.co.uk) or pop into the shop for some beer-related gifts. ⓐ Slad Lane, Woodbastwick ⓣ 01603 720003 ⓦ www.thefurandfeatherinn.co.uk ⓒ Bar: 09.00–22.30 Mon–Thur & Sun, 09.00–23.00 Fri & Sat; food: 09.00–21.00 Mon–Fri & Sun, 09.00–21.30 Sat

The Rising Sun ££ Watch the world go by as you sit by the river, admiring the wildlife, canoeists and tourist boats wind their way around the River Bure from the picnic benches outside The Rising Sun. There's another pub – The King's Head – as you enter the car park; or, if you just want to admire the view, the riverbank is a great place for a picnic. ⓐ 28 Wroxham Road, Coltishall ⓣ 01603 737440

The Wood's End ££ Perched on the banks of the River Yare, The Wood's End has an enviable location, which can be accessed by car, boat or, thanks to national cycle route number 1, by bike as well. Grab yourself a pint and take it down to the river for the perfect summer's evening. ⓐ Bramerton ⓣ 01508 538899

▶ *Clear signposting on the Norfolk Coast Path*

PRACTICAL
information

Directory

GETTING THERE

By air

Norwich International is 8km (5 miles) outside the city and is serviced by **Flybe**, which connects Norwich to other UK airports and a few European cities too. If you're arriving from further afield, then **KLM** is probably the best option.

Norwich International ⓐ Amsterdam Way ① 01603 411923 Ⓦ www.norwichairport.co.uk

Flybe Ⓦ www.flybe.com

KLM Ⓦ www.klm.com

Many people are aware that air travel emits CO_2, which contributes to climate change. You may be interested in the possibility of lessening the environmental impact of your flight through the charity **Climate Care** (Ⓦ www.jpmorgan climatecare.com) which offsets your CO_2 by funding environmental projects around the world.

By rail

Norwich Railway Station is a short walk from the city centre. **National Express East Anglia** currently hosts the London service and trains terminate their journey from London Liverpool Street here. Cambridge is just a short train ride away, and a great city to visit if you fancy a day outside of Norfolk. The local services to Sheringham, Cromer and Yarmouth are an ideal way to explore the coast if you don't have access to a car.

Norwich Railway Station ⓐ Station Approach

National Express East Anglia

Ⓦ www.nationalexpresseastanglia.com

The Trainline Ⓦ www.thetrainline.com

By road

National Express coaches from Birmingham-Coventry-Leicester, London and Gatwick-Heathrow-Stansted arrive into Norwich Bus Station. If you're coming via road by your own means, then you will probably approach the city centre by the A11 or A47.

Norwich Bus Station ⓐ Surrey Street and Queen's Road
ⓣ Traveline: 0871 200 2233 ⓛ Information desk: 08.00–18.00 Mon–Fri, 08.30–16.30 Sat, 10.00–14.00 Sun

National Express Ⓦ www.nationalexpress.com

Taxis

Thanks to its small size, Norwich is relatively easy to navigate on foot but it's not difficult to find a taxi if you want to give your feet a rest. The most central taxi rank is at Gaol Hill (outside Tesco Metro), and there are usually taxis waiting at the train station and Tombland.

HEALTH, SAFETY & CRIME

Norwich is a safe and friendly city but, like all other UK cities, it's important to take the usual precautions when visiting. During the day, you're unlikely to feel threatened or unsafe in any way. During weekend evenings, there's always a risk, as in any other town, of bumping into the odd drunkard. If you find yourself down Prince of Wales Road one evening and you're not part of one of the groups of revellers, then you may feel a bit overwhelmed by all the

drunken activity. But there's a strong police presence and you'll rarely feel unsafe. It's probably not wise, or necessary, to go through Chapelfield Gardens at night either.

OPENING HOURS

Shops and businesses are generally open between 09.00 and 17.30; however, on a Thursday evening some shops stay open until later (and almost all do in the run-up to Christmas) – taking closing time up to 20.00. The opening times of some of the independent shops may deviate from this pattern.

TOILETS

There are a handful of public toilets throughout the city but it's best to avoid these and instead use the facilities in one of the department stores. There are toilets at **Debenhams** (ⓐ Orford Place), **John Lewis** (ⓐ All Saints Green), **Marks & Spencer** (ⓐ Rampant Horse Street) and **Jarrold** (ⓐ London Street). If you're really desperate, it may be easier to nip into a pub unnoticed, rather than a café – but it's unlikely any establishment will be that impressed by your visiting just to use the toilets. Perhaps coincide your visit with a refreshment break, or at least ask politely.

CHILDREN

Children of all ages will enjoy visiting the castle and there are often special events put on during the school holidays – visit the website for more details. For hands-on learning, the **Inspire Discovery Centre** (ⓐ St Michael's Church, Oak Street ⓣ 01603 612612 ⓦ http://inspirediscoverycentre.com ⓛ Term time: 10.00–16.00 Mon–Fri, 11.00–17.00 Sun; school holidays: 10.00–17.00

daily) is a fun and interactive place and housed, seemingly randomly, in a church. The exhibits are linked to the national curriculum, but they are fun, accessible and a far cry from the classroom.

If you really want to treat the kids, then there are plenty of days out around Norfolk. At **BeWILDerwood** (ⓐ Horning Road, Hoveton ❶ 01603 783900 ⓦ www.bewilderwood.co.uk ⓔ explore@BeWILDerwood.co.uk) near Wroxham, enter a world full of magic, adventure, forest characters and bridges, boat trips and zip wires. If you like a forest setting, then Thetford Forest is about a 45-minute drive from the city. From the **High Lodge Forest Centre** (ⓐ off the B1107 Thetford to Brandon road ❶ 01842 815434 ⓦ www.forestry.gov.uk/highlodge) you can enjoy several walking trails, hire cycles and have fun in the play area. If you're feeling really adventurous there's also the opportunity to **Go Ape** (ⓦ www.goape.co.uk). And don't forget the coast is only a short drive away – just bring your bucket and spade.

TRAVELLERS WITH DISABILITIES

While the cobbled streets of Norwich are pretty to look at, unfortunately they can be a bit hard to traverse if you're in a wheelchair or have mobility difficulties. Luckily, there's plenty to see around the city and the main sites are accessible to travellers with disabilities.

FURTHER INFORMATION

For further information on Norwich and the surrounding areas visit ⓦ www.visitnorwich.co.uk and ⓦ www.visitnorfolk.co.uk

ACKNOWLEDGEMENTS

The photographs in this book were taken by Paul Walters for Thomas Cook Publishing, to whom the copyright belongs.

Project editor: Tom Willsher
Copy editor: Jennifer Jahn
Layout: Paul Queripel
Proofreaders: Penny Isaac & Ceinwen Sinclair
Indexer: Marie Lorimer

AUTHOR BIOGRAPHY

Stints of studying and travelling aside, Lucy Armstrong has called Norfolk home for most of her life. Living just outside the city centre, she's familiar – and fond of – everything Norwich has to offer. Beyond the city limits, she loves the Norfolk coast – especially Horsey in winter when the seal pups are on the beach.

Send your thoughts to
books@thomascook.com

- Found a great bar, club, shop or must-see sight that we don't feature?
- Like to tip us off about any information that needs a little updating?
- Want to tell us what you love about this handy little guidebook and more importantly how we can make it even handier?

Then here's your chance to tell all! Send us ideas, discoveries and recommendations today and then look out for your valuable input in the next edition of this title.

Email the above address (stating the title) or write to:
pocket guides Series Editor, Thomas Cook Publishing, PO Box 227, Coningsby Road, Peterborough PE3 8SB, UK.